Croley
NO AR

D0608374

Toussaint L'Ouverture

LOVER OF LIBERTY

Croley

Toussaint L'Ouverture

LOVER OF LIBERTY

by Laurence Santrey
illustrated by Gershom Griffith

Troll Associates

Copyright © 1994 by Troll Associates.

Illustrations copyright © 1994 by Gershom Griffith.

All rights reserved. No part of this book may be used or
reproduced in any manner whatsoever without written
permission from the publisher.

Printed in the United States of America.

10 9 8 7 6 5 4 3 2 1

Toussaint L'Ouverture

LOVER OF LIBERTY

What a great book! Toussaint thought. The words almost leaped off the page. "The two armies approached each other, the Trojans shouting like a huge flock of birds, the Greeks in grim silence. About their feet the dust rose, thick as mist in the mountains. As the forces came close enough to do battle—"

Whack! The book was knocked from the boy's hands. Startled, twelve-year-old Toussaint looked up at the man blocking his way.

"Sir, what is wrong?" Toussaint stammered.

"I'll tell you what's wrong, slave-boy! That book is stolen property. You must have taken it from your master."

"Oh, no, it was given to me by Father Luxembourg."

"Don't you dare lie to me, boy!" the man snarled. "You can't read. You're a slave."

"Oh, sir, I *can* read." Toussaint was proud of his education. "Here, I'll show you."

As the boy reached down to pick up the book, another blow of the stick sent him sprawling. He lay on the ground, helpless, as the man continued to beat him.

"That will teach you to keep your place." The man walked away, muttering angrily.

Toussaint sat on the ground, holding back tears of fury and shame. Slowly he stood and walked home. The pain was gone in a few days. But the memory of his helplessness as a slave stayed with Toussaint all his life.

Slavery was the terrible curse of Haiti from the time the first Europeans landed on its shores. When Christopher Columbus reached the island of Hispaniola in December 1492, he said, "This is the most beautiful place in all the world." But the Spanish conquerors who came to Hispaniola destroyed the paradise Columbus had found. They enslaved the natives and treated them worse than animals.

In 1697, France took the western part of the island from Spain and named it Haiti. The French created large plantations to produce sugar, coffee, and cocoa. Then they brought in slaves from Africa to work the land.

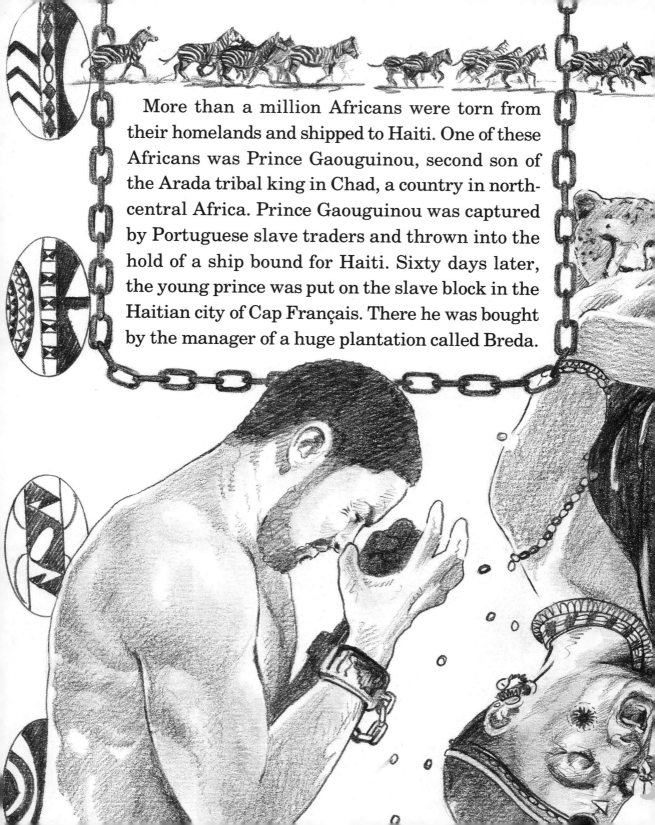

More than a million Africans were torn from their homelands and shipped to Haiti. One of these Africans was Prince Gaouguinou, second son of the Arada tribal king in Chad, a country in north-central Africa. Prince Gaouguinou was captured by Portuguese slave traders and thrown into the hold of a ship bound for Haiti. Sixty days later, the young prince was put on the slave block in the Haitian city of Cap Français. There he was bought by the manager of a huge plantation called Breda.

The French count who owned Breda gave his manager, Mr. Beager, full authority to run the plantation. He had just one unusual instruction: Treat the slaves as human beings.

Mr. Beager gave small parcels of land to many of the slaves on Breda. These were like small family farms where slaves were able to have their own homes and raise families. It wasn't total freedom, but it was better than the lives of most other slaves in Haiti.

Prince Gaouguinou was given one of these farms. He was also given a privilege called the Liberty of the Plantation. This meant he was a free man, so long as he stayed on the plantation. Since the plantation stretched for many miles, the "liberty" wasn't like being locked in a prison cell. But it still was not true freedom.

Soon after Prince Gaouguinou settled on his farm, he married a young woman from his own tribe. Their first child, François Dominique Toussaint, was born in 1743. His godfather, Pierre Baptiste Simon, was a freed slave who was a good friend of Prince Gaouguinou. He worked at a local hospital run by the priests, and acted as an advisor to the local people. Mr. Simon gave the child the name Toussaint, which is French for "all saints."

Toussaint was such a frail baby that his parents were afraid he would die. Mr. Simon used the medical skills he had learned at the hospital to keep Toussaint alive. But the boy was often sick when he was young. His friends nicknamed him "Little Stick" because he was so small and thin.

Toussaint was a very intelligent child, always eager to learn new things. Mr. Simon saw this and set out to teach him how to read and write in French and Latin. He also taught Toussaint arithmetic, French history, science, and some medicine.

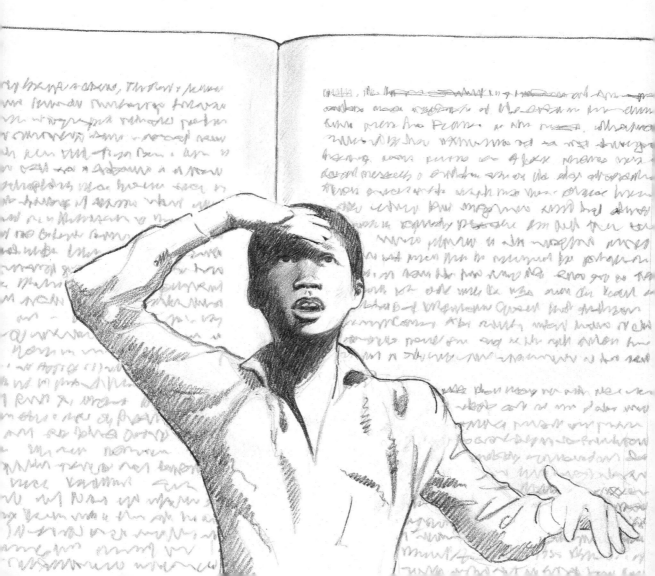

Mr. Simon often took the boy with him when he went to work at the hospital. Father Luxembourg, head of the hospital, was very impressed by young Toussaint. He allowed the boy to have free use of the priests' library. Toussaint stayed there for hours at a time, reading books about many different subjects.

Toussaint's education was very unusual. Most slave children were given no schooling. The plantation owners considered it very dangerous for their slaves to learn anything. The people who ran Haiti felt that education for the slaves was a threat to the rulers of the island.

Sometimes young Toussaint complained when Mr. Simon gave him a hard book to read. It was much more fun to go outside and play with his brothers and sisters or the other kids on the plantation.

"Julius Caesar!" he wailed one morning. "Why do I have to read a book by some silly old Roman soldier who died more than a thousand years ago? And in Latin, too!"

"Caesar was a great general and a wise leader," Mr. Simon answered. "He wrote long ago and in a different country, that is true. But the ways of the world do not change. And people do not change much, either. You can learn many things from Caesar's words."

"Can I be a great leader, Uncle Pierre?"

"Who can say?" Mr. Simon told the boy. "But one thing is certain—Haiti needs a patriot to lead it."

"Then I will be that leader. I will free all the slaves. I will be good and kind and wise." Toussaint grinned. "And I'll make every other day a holiday."

"Well, for now," Mr. Simon said, laughing, "just read your book. We'll worry about holidays later."

The boy read "Caesar's Commentaries," and learned much from them. And over and over again he read a history of the ruling empires of Europe. This book taught him a great deal about the economics and politics of the European countries. It also taught him how other countries ruled their colonies, compared to the way France ruled Haiti.

Toussaint studied a lot, but he didn't spend all his time with books. There were chores to be done on the family farm. Toussaint fed the chickens, helped tend the family's two goats, and weeded the garden. When work was done, there was time for play. Toussaint was a small, thin boy, but he grew stronger as he got older. In fact, Toussaint became the best athlete of all the children on the plantation. The boy loved to swim, climb trees and rocks, run races, and wrestle. He was shorter than others his age, but that only made him compete harder. "I am the little stick," he liked to say, "that beats every other kid around!" And he was right.

In the evenings, after his chores were done, Toussaint liked to listen to his father talk about Africa. Prince Gaouguinou told stories about the Arada tribe, about hunting in the forest, and about how tribal wars were fought. Gaouguinou did not want his children to forget their roots, so he also taught them to speak and understand the Arada language.

In later years, when Toussaint was a military leader, his knowledge of the Arada language and ways won him the loyalty and support of all the Aradas in Haiti. Since the Aradas were brave warriors, they supplied a strong backbone for his army.

Toussaint learned another important skill when he was still a boy. One of his jobs on the Breda plantation was helping to care for the horses. When Mr. Beager, the plantation manager, saw how well Toussaint worked, he was very pleased. So when the boy asked permission to ride the horses, the manager said, "Certainly. As long as you continue to do such good work, you may take a horse out any time you want to."

From then on, Toussaint went riding every day. Whenever there was an errand to town or a near-by plantation, the youngster eagerly offered to ride there. In time Toussaint became an expert horseman. In later years his horsemanship was one of the skills his followers admired about him. When Toussaint charged into battle, no soldier could fail to follow!

At the age of fifteen, Toussaint was put in charge of all the livestock on the plantation. He also became the supervisor of the many people who tended the animals. The young man was respected by the slaves, and was spoken to politely by the masters.

But Toussaint didn't forget that he was a slave himself. The Liberty of the Plantation that his father had been given years before was not really liberty. It was a cruel joke.

Prince Gaouguinou was sure his hard work and the Liberty of the Plantation protected him and his family. He was wrong. He learned this when one of his daughters was sold to another plantation owner. She was just a little girl, and she wept in terror as she was taken from her parents' small cabin.

Toussaint's mother lost her will to live when her youngest child was sold. She died soon after. Gaouguinou never recovered from the loss of his wife and his little girl. He died less than a year later. These terrible events showed Toussaint the true horror of slavery.

Now Toussaint, at the age of seventeen, was head of the family. He had to take care of his two younger brothers, Pierre and Paul, and a sister, Marie Noël. He knew that his boyhood was over.

From that day on, Toussaint set out to become very valuable to the plantation manager. He wanted to be seen as absolutely necessary for the plantation's success. This was the best way to protect his brothers, his sister, and himself.

Toussaint was clever, hard-working, and even-tempered. These qualities, plus his skill with horses, won him the position of personal coachman to the manager. It was a good job that left him with spare time every day. He used this time to tend to his family farm, and to teach his brothers and sister to read and write. He also made sure to save some hours for himself. He spent these studying history, military tactics, and politics.

The changes taking place in the American colonies excited Toussaint. He read about the colonists' demands for self-rule. He agreed with the great French thinkers, who said all people have natural rights. These ideas made Toussaint believe change was possible everywhere—even in Haiti. He was convinced that slavery must end on the island. It wasn't time yet, but Toussaint meant to be ready when that day came!

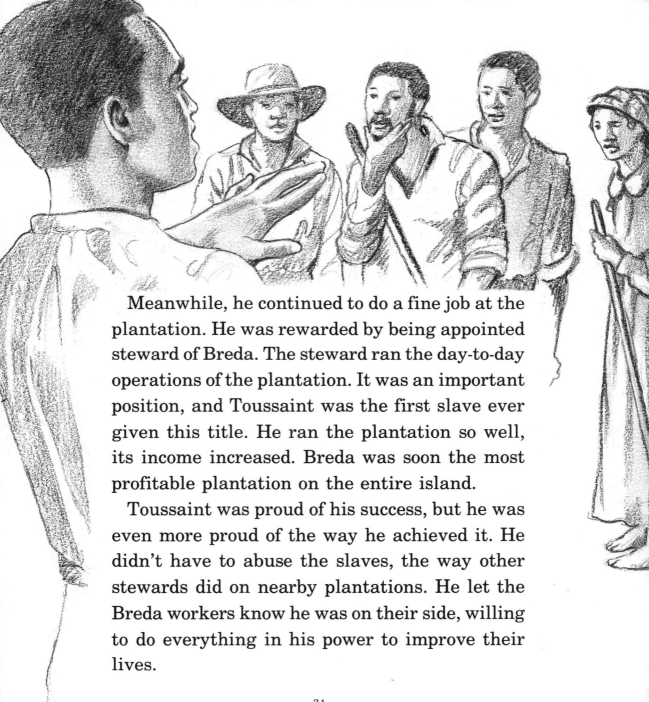

Meanwhile, he continued to do a fine job at the plantation. He was rewarded by being appointed steward of Breda. The steward ran the day-to-day operations of the plantation. It was an important position, and Toussaint was the first slave ever given this title. He ran the plantation so well, its income increased. Breda was soon the most profitable plantation on the entire island.

Toussaint was proud of his success, but he was even more proud of the way he achieved it. He didn't have to abuse the slaves, the way other stewards did on nearby plantations. He let the Breda workers know he was on their side, willing to do everything in his power to improve their lives.

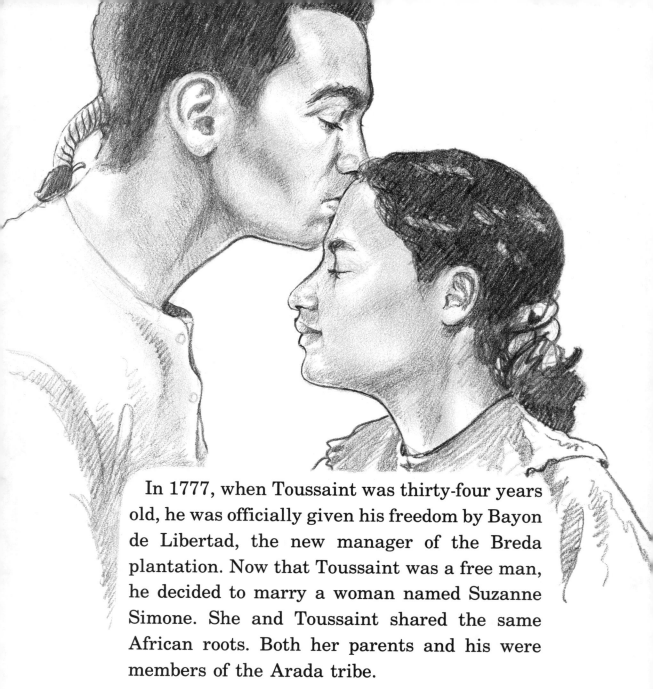

In 1777, when Toussaint was thirty-four years old, he was officially given his freedom by Bayon de Libertad, the new manager of the Breda plantation. Now that Toussaint was a free man, he decided to marry a woman named Suzanne Simone. She and Toussaint shared the same African roots. Both her parents and his were members of the Arada tribe.

Madame Simone already had a four-year-old son, Placide. The Toussaints had two more sons, Isaac and St. Jean. Toussaint was a very good father and husband. As he wrote years later, "Until the outbreak of the Revolution, I was never separated from my wife for any length of time. We worked side by side in our little garden, holding hands as we went to and from our work."

Toussaint's own life was happy, but he still dreamed of a Haiti free of slavery. The American Revolution fascinated him. He was overjoyed when the colonists won independence from England.

In 1789, the French people began their own revolution. They overthrew King Louis the Sixteenth. Then they declared France a republic, with elected officials. Some of the noblemen in France were killed. Others were jailed or forced to flee the country. Their great estates in France were taken from them.

French nobles who owned plantations on Haiti were afraid of losing them. But the slaves on Haiti were happy about the French Revolution. It held out the promise of freedom for them, too. They hoped the new French government would outlaw slavery.

This did not happen. Instead, the government freed only one group—people of mixed black and white parentage. This ruling had a crushing effect on the black slaves. They realized that the only way to win freedom was to fight for it.

The Haitian rebellion began in 1791. A Jamaican-born black named Boukmann led a band of slaves in an attack against the plantations. They swept across the land, burning crops and killing property owners and their families. There was real cause for rebellion, but Boukmann was more interested in revenge than freedom. Toussaint, who had hoped for a free Haiti, refused to join in this kind of bloody behavior.

Toussaint chose to join other patriots in a movement for justice, liberty, and equality. It was a time of war and confusion. All of Haiti became a battleground, with different groups fighting for control of the island. One group wanted Haiti to stay a French colony, ruled by white people and served by black slaves. Another group wanted to rid Haiti of all white people. A third group wanted freedom and civil rights for whites and people of mixed race—but not for blacks.

Toussaint led a group that wanted an independent country with freedom and equal rights for people of all races. In many ways, Toussaint's goal was the most revolutionary of all. He was far ahead of his time. He declared that "a country cannot truly be called free unless *everyone* in it is free." Toussaint hated racism—it was wrong no matter which group ruled and which group was enslaved.

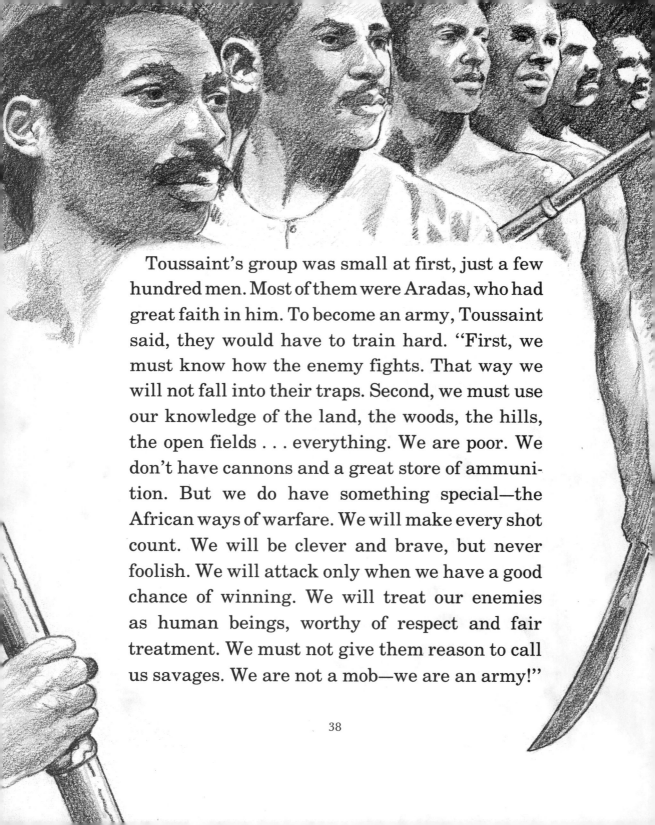

Toussaint's group was small at first, just a few hundred men. Most of them were Aradas, who had great faith in him. To become an army, Toussaint said, they would have to train hard. "First, we must know how the enemy fights. That way we will not fall into their traps. Second, we must use our knowledge of the land, the woods, the hills, the open fields . . . everything. We are poor. We don't have cannons and a great store of ammunition. But we do have something special—the African ways of warfare. We will make every shot count. We will be clever and brave, but never foolish. We will attack only when we have a good chance of winning. We will treat our enemies as human beings, worthy of respect and fair treatment. We must not give them reason to call us savages. We are not a mob—we are an army!"

Toussaint's men soon became excellent soldiers. The army's training and Toussaint's leadership were proved in the battle of Morne Pélé.

Morne Pélé, a hill near the city of Cap Français, was a key position because it overlooked the harbor, the city, and the surrounding countryside. The French attacked the hill day and night, and had defeated one Haitian force after another. Then Toussaint and his army were sent to hold the position.

Toussaint directed the fierce battle on horseback. When he saw the French general riding close by, Toussaint drew his sword and challenged the other officer.

The two men fought bitterly, the clanging of their swords ringing above the sounds of battle. It was a close contest until Toussaint was cut on the right arm. His troops, seeing their leader wounded, showed signs of doubt. And the French soldiers surged forward, up the hill.

Toussaint swiftly pulled the gold general's sash from around his waist. He wrapped it over his shoulder and around his right arm, making a sling. Then, gripping his sword, Toussaint roared, "Follow me, brave patriots!" and led a charge against the enemy. The French were no match for the inspired Haitians. They were driven back down the hill in defeat. This victory was a turning point for Haitian freedom and for Toussaint's leadership.

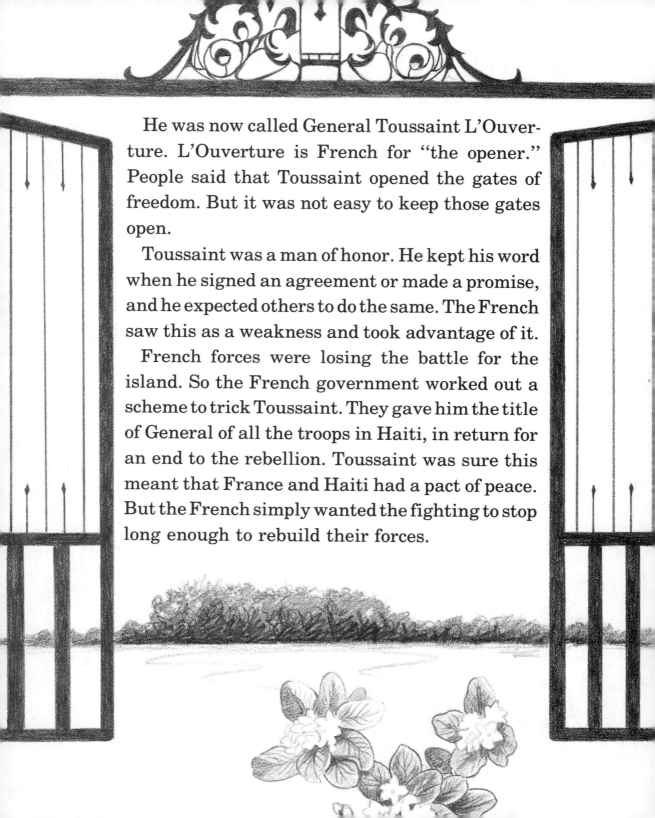

He was now called General Toussaint L'Ouverture. L'Ouverture is French for "the opener." People said that Toussaint opened the gates of freedom. But it was not easy to keep those gates open.

Toussaint was a man of honor. He kept his word when he signed an agreement or made a promise, and he expected others to do the same. The French saw this as a weakness and took advantage of it.

French forces were losing the battle for the island. So the French government worked out a scheme to trick Toussaint. They gave him the title of General of all the troops in Haiti, in return for an end to the rebellion. Toussaint was sure this meant that France and Haiti had a pact of peace. But the French simply wanted the fighting to stop long enough to rebuild their forces.

In 1801, Toussaint declared Haiti a republic, and he became its first president. He established schools, because he believed that free people needed education. The Haitian people had to learn to be free citizens, be able to run businesses, publish newspapers, vote for their own officials, and do all the other things a free people are expected to do. Education was the key.

Toussaint also knew that Haiti's real strength lay in farming. He often said, "When we can feed ourselves, we need not eat out of the hand of any other person on earth. Did we not fill the treasure chests of other nations with the fruits of our soil? Now we can use our rich land for ourselves."

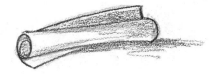

President Toussaint set an ideal example for his people. He lived simply and honorably. His fame spread throughout the world. President John Adams of the United States was deeply impressed by Toussaint's wise leadership. Adams was pleased to sign a trade agreement with Haiti. England followed the example of the United States and signed its own trade agreement with Haiti.

Napoleon Bonaparte, the ruler of France, was not pleased by all this. He did not care if the Haitians thought their country was independent. But it was very bad for France if Haiti was accepted as an independent country by others. Napoleon decided that things had gone too far. He sent a large military force to take over the island. The French defeated the Haitians on May 1, 1802. Toussaint surrendered to spare his people from more suffering and death. But he did so only after France promised peace and fair treatment to Haiti.

It was another trick. Toussaint was told to give up his leadership and retire to his farm, where no harm would come to him. He accepted—and was betrayed by Napoleon. The trusting Toussaint was arrested and taken to France, where he was thrown into prison. He died there on April 27, 1803. It was a sad day for Haiti, and for lovers of freedom everywhere.

In the short time Toussaint led Haiti, he wasn't able to create a lasting, free republic. But he did give his people a sense of hope and dignity. The heritage that Toussaint gave to Haiti—honor, courage, goodness, a yearning for freedom—continues to this day. For centuries Haiti's people have suffered more than their share of misery. Unfortunately, that misery remains today. But, with the dreams of Toussaint in mind, Haitians of good will have not given up.

François Dominique Toussaint L'Ouverture was called one of the most remarkable men in an age of remarkable men. Born a slave, he became a symbol of freedom. To this day his name lives on wherever people struggle for liberty.

INDEX